PIANO PIECES & PUZZLES

I0798707

Level One

Music and Lyrics by Al Rita and Dan Rita
Activities created and illustrated by Jocelyn Rita

Foreword

This unique series will intrigue and motivate your students to better musical accomplishment. Each book combines progressive piano solos with an activity coordinated with every piece. The lyrics express a wholesome outlook toward personal and social experiences, and the environment.

Enhanced educational value is found in many activities which involve music notation and musical terms. Activities are designed to appeal to a range of ages appropriate to the musical level.

It is suggested that the music be learned first, using the activity as an incentive to finish the music.

Schaum Publications, Inc.
10235 N. Port Washington Rd. • Mequon, WI 53092
www.schaumpiano.net

13-06
LB-1

Swinging

Music by Al Rita
Words by Dan Rita

Cantabile ♩= 132-144

17
Sky up a - bove, the ground be - low, as
p
21
free as a bird I go.
25
Up in the air, I don't have a care. I
mf
29
swing my wor - ries a - way.
rit.
p

Swinging Cypher

Use the measures below to decode each word.

SWIN +  = ______________

BR + 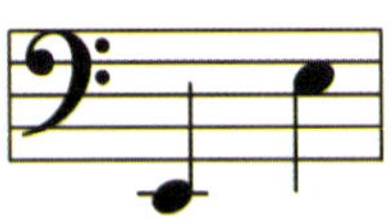 + ZE = ______________

LIM +  + S = ______________

 + OVE = ______________

 + LOW = ______________

 + REE = ______________

BIR +  = ______________

 + WAY = ______________

TR +  + S = ______________

L +  + VES = ______________

PUZZLING PARADE

Search the parade for these nine hidden music symbols: treble clef, bass clef, staccato note, forte, mezzo piano, mezzo forte, crescendo, diminuendo, and fermata.

Big Parade

Music by Al Rita
Words by Dan Rita

Alla marcia ♩= 138-160

17
Ev - 'ry girl and boy, they all shout out with joy. They're
p
21
cheer - ing on the big pa - rade. See the
f
25
flags and stream - ers fly, lead - ing on the mo - tor - cade. Come with
29
us a - long the way, join - ing in the big pa - rade.

How Carrie Got Merry

Music by Al Rita
Words by Dan Rita

Allegretto ♩= 138-152

Scaredy Cat

Select eight of the keyboard pawprints to write a scary tune for Carrie's cat to play. The notes can be in any order. Write four quarter notes in the bass staff and four in the treble staff. Use an accidental sharp or flat for the black keys. When you are finished, play your scary tune.

World of Surprise

Music by Al Rita
Words by Dan Rita

21
4
not a cloud in sight, it seems the world
2
26
2 1
sings ev - 'ry song for you.
31
5 3
And they all ring true. O - pen your mind. Look what you'll
mf
36
2 1 2
find. The world is wait - ing for you!
f

Musical Matches

Draw a line to match each note to its correct key on the keyboard.

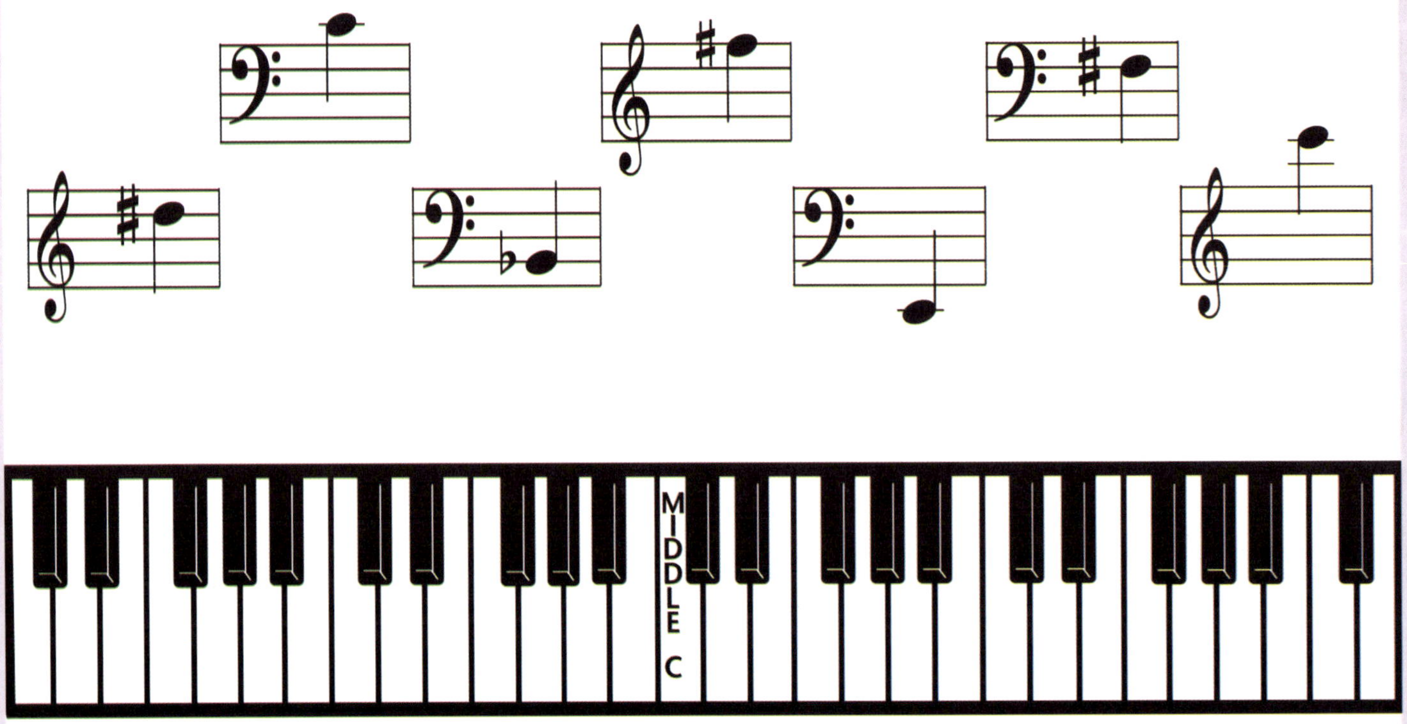

Time for Friends

Complete the time signatures for the measures below. Then draw a picture of yourself and a special friend in the frame.

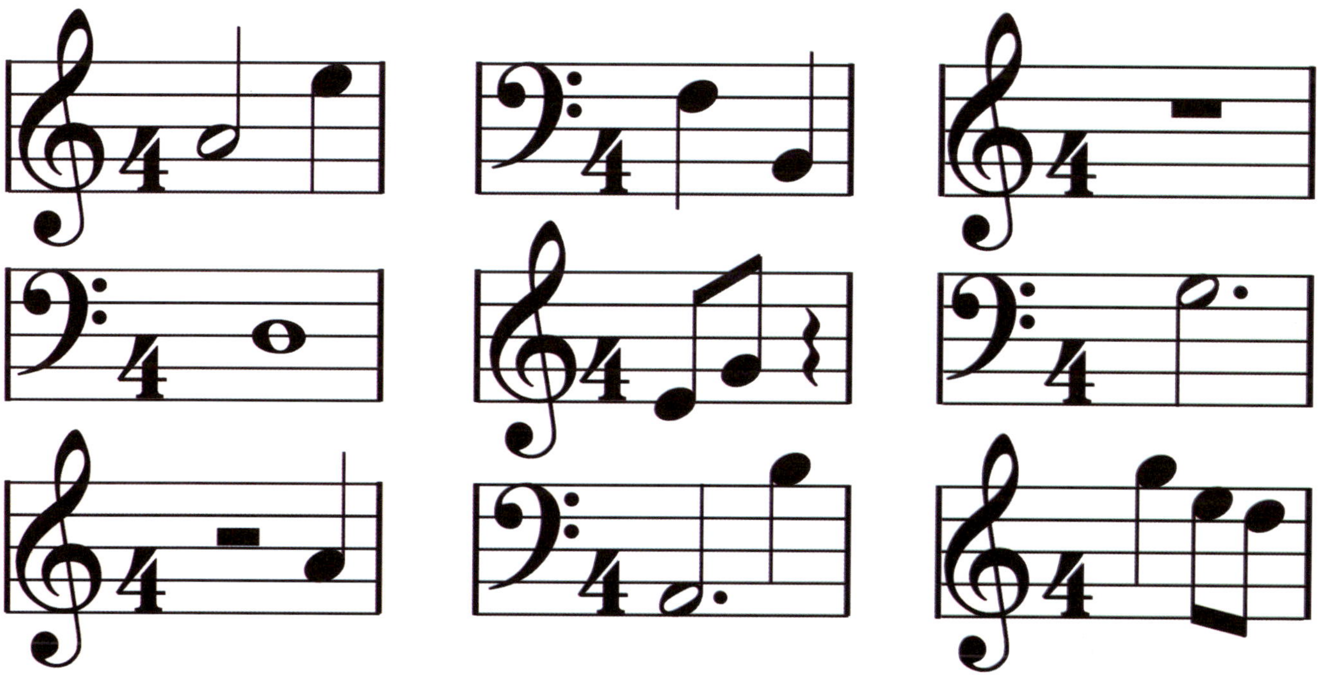

A Friend Is a Friend

Music by Al Rita
Words by Dan Rita

Allegretto ♩ = 126–144

cats, and the kids all think he's cool. A friend is a
friend, is a friend. No mat - ter who you
are or what you wear. An - y friend who can lift you
up is a friend be - yond com - pare.
rit.

Go-Go Flamingo

Words and music by Al Rita

Flamingo Fun

Determine which musical terms fit each picture below.
Write the letter of the matching picture next to each musical term.
The first one is done for you.

1. forte __A__
2. largo ______
3. andante ______
4. staccato ______
5. piano ______
6. allegro ______
7. crescendo ______
8. pianissimo ______
9. fortissimo ______
10. diminuendo ______

A

B

My Favorite Sport

Alla marcia ♩= 152–176

Words and music by Al Rita

17
2
4
Who will score a touch-down, or make the win-ning play?
f
21
2
2
1
On-ly time will tell, 'til then no-one can say.
25
2
4
Win or lose, no mat-ter, it's how you play the game. My
29
2
2
fav-'rite sport is foot-ball! It's so much fun to play!
ff
1

Football Funjumble

Unjumble the musical terms below to score a touchdown for Piano U!

Piano U

raqetur ______________

mseruea ______________

reebtl ______________

hlowe ______________

hrspa ______________

rotfe ______________

opani ______________

eotn ______________

alft ______________

sbsa ______________

Organ State

Silly Scene

There are 15 silly things in the picture below. See if you can find them all.

Silly Song

Music by Al Rita
Words by Dan Rita

Allegro ♩= 152-176

(optional) **Make up your own words for a 3rd verse, in measures 10 through 18:**

Make it ____________________ Make it ____________________ Make it ____________________

Make it ____________________ Make it ____________________ Make it ____________________

Things I Like a Lot

Words and music by Al Rita

Symbol Crossword

Use the word bank below to solve this musical crossword puzzle

fortissimo	sharp	half
crescendo	flat	piano
staccato	signature	forte
treble	eighth	dotted
bass	quarter	natural

ACROSS

3. ____ half note
4. time ____
5. ♭
6. 𝆒
9. ♪ note
11. 𝄽 rest
12. *p*
13. 𝄢
14. *f*

DOWN

1. *ff*
2. 𝅗𝅥 note
4. ♩.
7. ♮
8. ♯
10. 𝄞

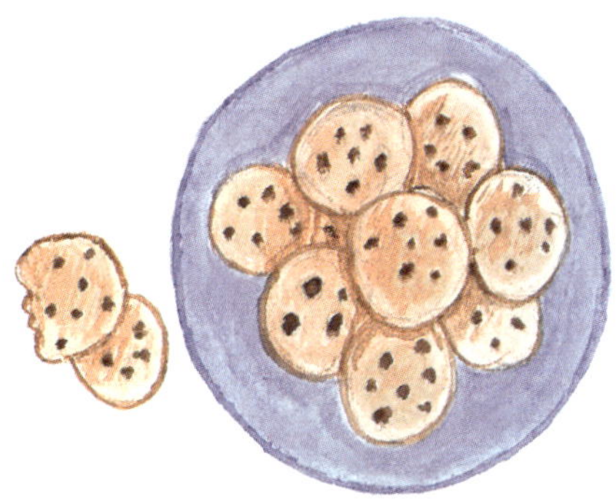

Splish Splash Swimming Pool

Music by Al Rita
Words by Dan Rita

Giocoso ♩ = 112-126

Splish Splash

Look up, down, forward, backward and diagonally for the words below.

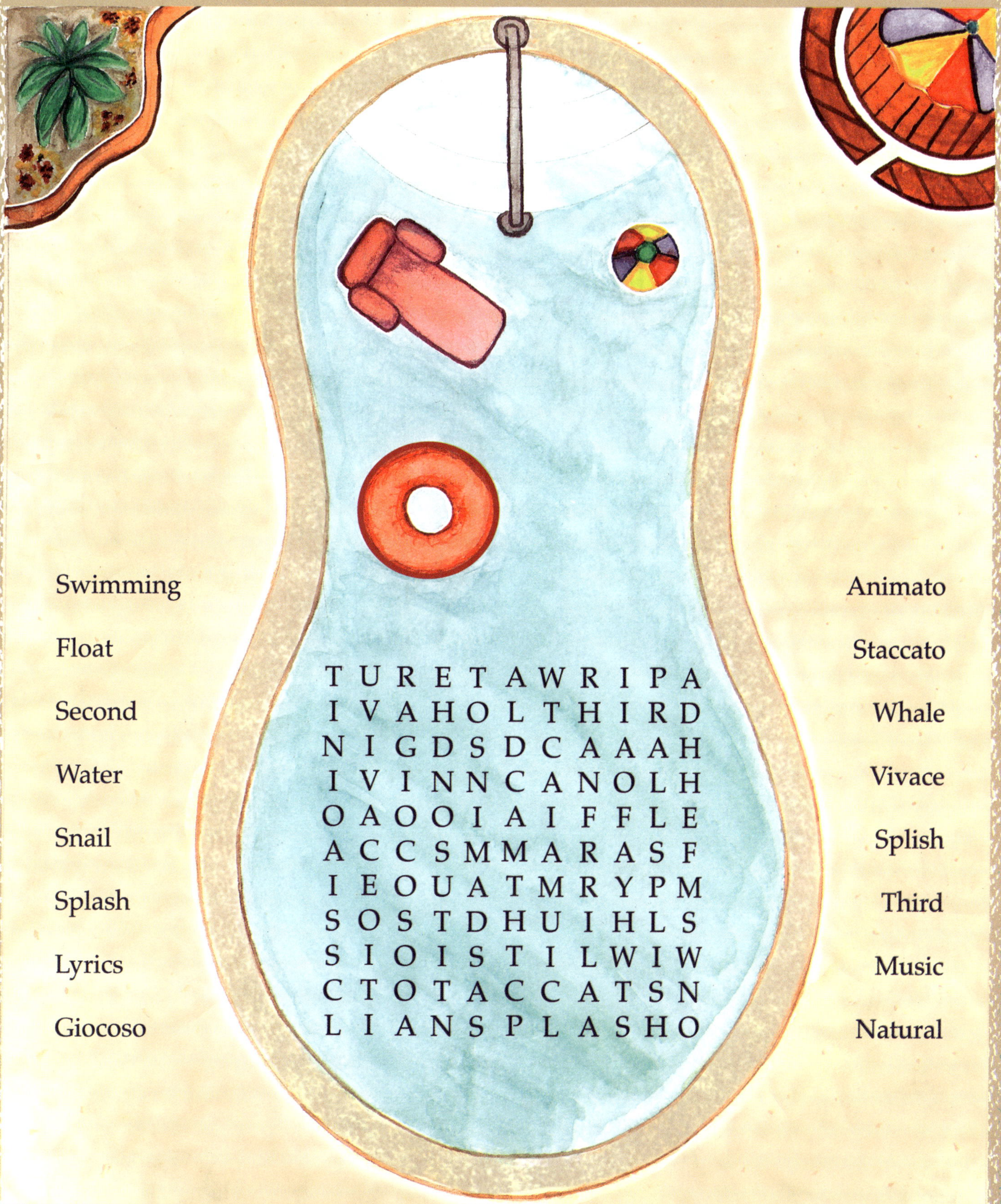

```
T U R E T A W R I P A
I V A H O L T H I R D
N I G D S D C A A A H
I V I N N C A N O L H
O A O O I A I F F L E
A C C S M M A R A S F
I E O U A T M R Y P M
S O S T D H U I H L S
S I O I S T I L W I W
C T O T A C C A T S N
L I A N S P L A S H O
```

Swimming
Float
Second
Water
Snail
Splash
Lyrics
Giocoso

Animato
Staccato
Whale
Vivace
Splish
Third
Music
Natural

Starfish Wish

Connect the dots and then use your imagination to color in this underwater world.

Does a Starfish Make a Wish?

Music by Al Rita
Words by Dan Rita

* *Stars in the sea* refers to starfish.

Squirrels In the Trees

Music by Al Rita
Words by Dan Rita

Vivo ♩ = 108-126

9
scur - ry through the yard and Red throws a fit.
11
They like to play tag, but Red is al - ways "it."
13
Lis - ten to them chat - ter with a CHEE, CHEE, CHEE!
15
Lis - ten to the squirrels in the tree, tree, tree! CHEE! CHEE! CHEE!

Pesky Pals

Make your way through the maze by using the two measures of music below. Every time you reach a set letters, make sure to choose the path that matches the next note on the staff. Be sure to pay attention to how each note is written on the staff!